Oct. '18

To Carmela,
It is due to friends, that in the best of times swim along side us joyfully; in the worst of times, when sea currents can be unbearable, they keep us buoyant.
Thank you for being my friend.

DISTANT BORDERS

Maria Keeney

DISTANT BORDERS

A FEATHER IN THE BREADTH AND FLOW

TRAVEL POETRY
BY
MARIA KEENEY

Copyright © 2018 by Maria Keeney
All rights reserved. This book or any portion thereof
may not be reproduced or used in any manner whatsoever
without the express written permission of the publisher
except for the use of brief quotations in a book review.
Instagram:suitcase_poet
Twitter:Maria Keeney TunetoaNaturalE
Printed in Great Britain

First Print 2018

For Mark

'Travel is fatal to prejudice, bigotry, and narrow-mindedness, and many of our people need it sorely on these accounts. Broad, wholesome views of men and things cannot be acquired by vegetating in one little corner of the earth all one's lifetime.'

Mark Twain

Contents

Travel in Pantoum..3

For a Moment Run (Icelandic in Iceland)..................4

Dying Fishermen..6

The Winds Sway Willis..9

The Lake District (with introduction)......................10

Living in Italy..15

I Met Him in a Candy Box....................................16

Somewheres 'cross seven-united states.................. 19

Maschere del Carnivale (Sardinia, Italy)..................20

Cocoon it in Finland...22

Hot Air Balloon...24

Settle in Cimarron..26

It's Hot Here in Cancun......................................28

Autumn Train to Wales..30

London is a Friend of Mine..................................32

Trust Alice...34

Freight Trains in Idaho..36

Hold Tight Dolomites..39

Neuschwanstein in the Clouds................................41

Hushpuppies and Grits..43

Where Golden Fields Rush Kansas.......................44

Open Market in Winchester..................................46

Bruges, Belgium..47

Modern Times in Ancient Egypt............................48

Sequoiadendron Giganteum..................................50

Venice Simplon-Orient-Express.............................51

Train Travel..54

Down the Mighty Mississippi.................................55

For Miss Honduras...56

Chantilly, France...59

Kayaking in Nova Scotia..60

Haiku for Holland...61

Wander On..62

Acknowledgements..65

THE POEMS

I VENTURE TO DISTANT BORDERS
I TRAVEL FOR A WANT TO SEE

Pantoum
noun /pæn'tum/ pantoum /panˑ'tüm/

Travel in Pantoum

I venture to distant borders
I travel for a want to see
I escape from boxed corners
I journey for my sanity

I travel for a want to see
I dare not live a stagnant life
I journey for my sanity
I want to be a bird in flight

I dare not live a stagnant life
I aim to drift like leaves in breeze
I want to be a bird in flight
I cannot live like rooted trees

I aim to drift like leaves in breeze
I escape from boxed corners
I cannot live like rooted trees
I venture to distant borders

For a Moment Run
(Icelandic in Iceland)

I ride an Icelandic at flying pace
and then at four-beat amble grace
when winter white's like crystal blush
and geysers rise from earthen crust
blasting water and spouting steam
where mounds of green lie in between.
Tryggur Icelandic upon the plain,
with russet coat and full thick mane,
take me for a fleeting run,
below cream skies of hidden sun.

Thermal waters of Blue Lagoon
glow in the brief-light afternoon
when wintertide is mainly dark
on landscape of few trees or bark.
Sparse populace means roaming free
is day adrift in reverie
where a name or age don't matter much
and ears hear mere patters of
rhythm of hooves and wind-whipped hair—
a moment's run alone foursquare.

*Passing fjords in nimble gait
to Gullfoss we will make our way
to massive sprays from waterfall
and arctic mountains godly tall,
we lope amidst sulphurous air
on Mars-like land where puffins share
crags and rocks hemmed in mossy seams
 'neath Aurora Borealis beams
where lithe Icelandic smoothly runs,
in to clear nights when chroma comes.*

*Unbound in Europe's last frontier
near lava deep and acres pure
and glaciers floating glassy-sheer,
Icelandic trots with fervour here
beyond small wooden pitched-roof homes
upon unspoilt nature honed
in spreads and sweeps all wide and wild
awakening the dormant child
of yester-moons and youthful sun—
Icelandic, for a moment run!*

Monday Edition - **Greek News** - 04/04/2017

Forgotten   Wooden   Boats

In Greece, proud men who are part of generations of fishermen angling from little wooden boats, are being pushed out of the sea by the big EU fishing industry. Fishermen are paid-off by these companies — paid for their boats they use for their livelihood—paid to 'make them disappear'. These men who've watched their grandfathers and fathers fish for decades — are one by one getting hooked by the EU industry. Fishermen of small Greek islands say they are ending up like the fish they've watched die. The majority of men feel hopelessness on land. The boats are extensions of the men's hearts—as if the timbre that braved the sea waters for years had a soul of its own. These days, for the small wooden boat fishermen in Greece, and much of Europe, there's limited work to make a decent living. New generations that had hoped to carry on fishing from a tiny wooden boat are now leaving the mainland and seeking alternative jobs or education. And for those opting to buy a new boat—it's most likely made of plastic.

Dying Fishermen

Saltwater had flecked, faded and jaded,
the fishermen caps sun-aged and braided,
that shaded Greek anglers browned on a boat
who downed sugared ouzo to coat their throats.
Their thick weathered hands flicked through the brine
then baited rusting hooks and cast off lines.
Those robust men thrusting poles and reeling
caught day's praised catch under blazing ceiling.
'If we don't fish the sea, we have no lives',
said men in wooden boats who strived to thrive
on old traditions now adrift and past,
'we barnacled watch big trawlers gaining fast'.
Coastlines are crawling with bright-whitewashed domes,
or swashed flat top views, or blue shuttered homes.
'Leave us and leave room for fish by and by.
When oceans are vacuumed, we all will die'.
There, foam flutters in Cyclades Islands,
and sea's surface shines like bouncing diamonds.
Dine on fish tales, feta and aubergine...
by the sublime azure Aegean Sea.

Cloud Gate - the bean shaped orb by Anish Kapoor

The Winds Sway Willis

Cotton candy is candyfloss, is Grandpa's beard, is sugar moss.
Bears are big but the Cubs are boss
when batting balls in Wrigley Field.

Chicago's windy—winds blow cold—winds tunnel through skyscraper rows.
Willis swayed while I Fly-girl posed
in a glass-deck over Illinois.

There's popcorn shrimp and pop-cult shoes popping up at the House of Blues.
Harmonicas screech Delta grooves
down brownstone Al Capone alleys.

Orb is parked in Millennium Park imparking views in mirrored arc.
Art Institute shows Basque, and barque,
and works by Cole, Wood, and Hopper.

There's no match for Frank Lloyd Wright, his unmatched homes and 'matching' wife
swathed wholly in tones: earth, fire and ice.
I toured Oak Park and Roloson Row.

On a walled corner, 'Corner's' resides where I ate four-cornered pie.
Hefty Peterbilts rumbled by
while I snacked on Mar's Castle cheese.

Tri-Rail chug-chugs through Kankakee—mugs of Pabst were chugged in Milwaukee.
Jackson Five's old home in Gary
was hardly larger than a shed.

Though the Heartland's landscape is flat, its inland has more heart than that:
Great Lakes, homey meals, porkpie hats—
and quilt-art atop Midwest barns.

Goodbye Hoosiers, bye star spangled band, bye-bye to wide dairy land.
I left O'Hare with bag in hand
alone on a morning flight home.

Resting up in Northern England, close to Scotland, is the Lake District—it's Wordsworth, and Beatrix Potter country. There was a peaceful place to stay; it was a fold—a hundred-year-old converted barn loft adjacent to a quaint cottage, in Hallin Bank overlooking Lake Ullswater. The area is quintessential northern British farm life. It's green country—in more ways than one. Enveloped in all things earthy, tucked in by the grassy covered enormity, homesteads almost appear to be born and blossomed from the fertile ground. Cottages are dotted far apart. Roofs and crannies are freckled in moss, meticulously trimmed with rosebushes or colourful flowers that stand-out against grey slate. The same slate is piled in a natural fashion and used for cottages, trailing walls, and walls sparsely running up, down, and over the green.

The walls—the cairns—have been a part of the landscape for centuries marking memorials, burial grounds, hilltops, and routes. Footpath advisors ask walkers to leave the stones; leave the wild as it is. Do not create 'art' in nature, or take a stone to place on the summit as a sign of achievement. Most people hope to get away from civilisation, and escape any form of graffiti, and surely find the art is in nature itself.

There are fourteen lakes, tangled trees, and endless rolling green fells for hiking—such as Hallin Fell. Deep breathing is an art there. The quiet is only interrupted by comforting sounds of nature, scattered sheep, cattle lowing, rivers babbling, or the metronomic water lapping against rocks. As for the rare manmade sounds—they're likely the soft steps of Wellies along free-for-all footpaths, or in the sounds of the gathering of gooseberries coming from fresh-faced rustic Cumbrians.

Take Nothing. Leave Nothing.

The Lake District

At the foot of Hallin Fell was a bench with a brass plaque:

'And when you have reached the mountain top, then you shall begin to climb.'

Kahlil Gibran

The Lake District

Not knowing which way to turn when I heard
(while lost, although not in a quagmire)
the crackling of gingerbread home fires,
and faint whispers from blankets of bluebells,
as I cast eyes on emerald fells
across the woolly ridden Lakeland.

                    I ambled, slowly tracing my steps back
                          to my rented dwelling full of coal,
          when Wordsworth's Dove Cottage cooed to soul-
              poets, it called as yester-morn started
                        to daisy-rise and I'd imparted
                    'lonely as a cloud' to gold clearings.

The north grows heather in broken weather
in Cumbria where stout Herdwick lambs
laik on Hill Top 'long Beatrix's land,
and irksome rabbits romp 'round fourteen lakes
near switches in swales that swish and quake
when red squirrels fine-comb and forage.

        Rams high on the peak, I'd reached Obelisk
                on Ullswater's Hallin Fell hike.
        And I'd heard of Dollywaggon Pike,
              or assessing an old anomaly
            like the photo of Tizzie-Whizie
     (the hedgehog-foxtail-bee-winged thing).

I'd trekked verdant paths of the nearby Dales
and was a distance from mountain tarns,
running fervent hands 'cross District cairns,
eating damsons like the kind in chutney,
gathering thankful agrimony—
in truth, I'd really not wandered far.

          I returned to the loft near the thicket
        where nature's breath was silvery mist,
       mingling with still pools in sleepiness—
      it was peace good enough to beckon me
      back to tumbling English fells and sheep,
        suggesting: *a week's stay is too brief.*

Many shops, and many businesses close for two hours each day. One is told to take to heart, *'To live in Italy means learning to enjoy unhurried time daily, with friends and family. It is essential that life not be consumed with work; this is why eating together is not just a meal...it's an event'*.

Living in Italy

At noonday there's a balmy breeze
and heat beats on the cortile,
steaming candlestick cypress trees
by my villa in Campoli.
The Sangiovese grapes are plump,
and scents of vino rosso leak
through a cellar of casks and aging meat,
to pigeon tower's peak.

Our priest in thirty-three-button cassock
has rosary in hand,
driving a Vespa past olive groves
to bless our home and land.
I watch him with his helmet on,
buzzing along on the scooter,
near sunny rows of rosemary,
where I wave to vineyard workers.

My boys play riffs on marble floors;
my girl studies First Communion.
The local cat lies by the gate—
'Tiberio', people call him.
Penne boils on my stove,
while Santa Maria's bells chime at dusk.
My husband makes his way back home,
to where life never seems a rush.

In blackness without a streetlight,
come ominous sounds that pain me:
wild boar grunting in deep night,
running through fields of Chianti.
Cries from distant deer captured,
twine with crickets and hoopoe trills.
Tuscany I'm ever enraptured,
in the haunting of your hills.

I Met Him in a Candy Box

At the Blackpool Funfair,
along the seafront there,
he's standing in a candy box.
The North Beach winds freeze,
and that's where palmists' read,
while he is selling candyfloss.

The Tower is Eiffel-like,
Stanley Park has pike,
and ballroom dancers fill the hall.
I strolled the Dune Grass Strand,
past donkey rides on sand,
past arcade bells and chippy stall.

In North-West Lancashire
see North, South, and Central piers,
and Sandgrown'uns fishing for sea bass.
In sticky carrel air,
I met a Romanian there,
spinning shreds of sugar glass.

The Fylde Coast stretches wide,
there's roller coaster rides,
and circus folk in frilly frocks.
He talked about young dreams,
away from Pleasure Beach,
escaping life near Cocker Clock.

Twirled me a cotton cone,
then told me with a groan,
'This is the town of Tangerines.
Life's more than football brats,
or wearing paper hats,
or being Tussaud's figurine'.

Cold ocean sprayed my skin;
wool collar cupped my chin.
Old Casino was up ahead.
As tram rolled slowly by,
I called to candy guy,
'I wish you best of luck', I said.

At the Blackpool Funfair,
along the seafront there,
he's standing in a candy box.
He said he's soon to leave
North Beach winds that freeze,
and coloured dyes of candyfloss.

A young man struggled to get through school. He made candyfloss to send money home to his family in Romania. He was alone in a tiny booth up in Northern England, near the Blackpool Tower that rises 500 feet over the sea.
Speaking in broken English he said,
'I'm not going to spend my life
standing in a candy box'.

*It felt effortless to fall
into an altered Southern accent.*
That homey appeal:
the lattice-top cherry pie's scent,
or the feel of Georgia peaches
all plump (some spent)
and fuzzy in filled buckets.
Empty porch swings
luring and inviting,
seemed to beam
with ease of simple things.
I did dream
and I slept
on that Chattanooga Choo-Choo train—
its kept cars remain
standing still
with its hushed whistle—
while the song of the same name
played and played.
And in fresh pancake-rise comfort of morning
near berry bushes in webbed dawning,
when country birds came calling,
I climbed above the waterfall
there at Rock City...
where seven states lay before me
in glory of Southern scenery
teeming with life up and under—
consumed with curiosity and wonder.

Somewheres 'Cross Seven-United States
(In Rock City)

Aint gonna be no need fo' crispy fried
   chicken pot pie past Flat Top Ridge
      an' no lard-pastry cherry pie tasty
         'bove gnomes, waterfall, crick, o' bridge.
What matters is seein' Black-Eyed Susan
   slippin' down sloped hills of scene'ry
      with seven southun states laid 'cross them plains
         split 'tween acres of trees an' green'ry.
Them signs on red-barn rooftops are found
   scattered 'round the motherland, **See Rock City**—
      in black an' white in big bold letters
         o' on birdhouses that're itty bitty.
There're gardens an' crystals inside caves
   an' a tight-fit through Fat Man Squeeze,
      in the original land of Coca-Cola
         where Butterfly Weed is shor ta please.

On the high lookout point called Lover's Leap
   at the peak of the rise in Rock City
      where Tennessee meets Georgia peach
         them sights're awful perty.
Good ol' Kentucky boys are somewheres
   shootin' tin cans inside that span
      an' Virginni farm hans are drivin'
         John Deeres up an' down their land.
Belles of the Carolinas jus' might
   be sittin' on Adirondack swings
      while an Alabama mama tends
         ta young 'uns on her apron strings.
Aint gonna be no need fo' cash o' jewels
   o' fancy duds o' spit-shined shoes
      'cause it's 'bout open views an' trails
         an' seein' neon Mother Goose.
Somewheres 'cross seven-united states
   near Chattanooga is Rock City.
      Go ta sleep on the choo-choo train
         then go see sights that're awful perty.

Maschere del Carnivale—Sardegna
(Carnival of Masks—Sardinia, Italy)

Quiet roads down rows of gold broom Genista trees. I was pleased
by their most intoxicating honey scent. So fragrant -
it lingered on and I let it penetrate. Saturate.

High upon a rock the island's castle breathed mirth. Perched,
above bluest Mediterranean Sea. See and believe,
in an ancient legacy befallen. It's calling

to Mamoiada, and Oristano, and much more. Folklore
and customs, and caped masked-men on horses race, to chase
a star and pierce it, expressionless. With expressiveness

each region has its own take and variants. Merriment
fills the streets with components of pagan rites. That night
the moon looked slightly like papier-mâché. We found our way

up to windy Castelsardo's carnival. Annual
treats were rolled, baked, and sugared. With vigour
we caught donuts being tossed out of trucks, for luck.

Wild festoons trimmed allegoric carriages. Narratives
and mockeries in Italian were made. The blades
of sharp silly tongues poked fun at politics. They're critics.

Sardinia is a small world all on its own. And sown,
are seeds of tribal drums beating heavily. Ebony
was the eve's sort-of-foreboding summer sky. Dark eyes

peered from wooden animal masks that haunted. They taunted,
and teased, and brown dancers wore headdress and grass.
People passed candies and threw a ton of confetti. We were ready.

It rocked, it smacked, it had *thunderous pounds*. Booming sounds
like I'd never heard, but hope to hear again! And when
seven hundred twenty pounds of cowbells rang, it was *roaring*!

Robust posse, pile on sheepskin once a year. Adhere!
Those herded Mamuthones pace in procession. Possession:
to be roped by Issahadores brings wishes. Auspicious.

It's a two-thousand-year-old ritual scene. Come glean
from mysterious ones that have carried on, and are drawn
to fulfilling their duties and traditions. Now listen.

Their hefty steps are steady and powerful. Artful.
Twelve men struck a man-animal connection. Bless them.
Watch parallel lines as they plod together. Good measure.

In Sardinian cities they will appear. Don't fear
deep baritone chants, stomps, and *heavy grunts*. No affronts!
Yes…there are still things that go bump in the night. Delight!

The Carnival of Masks is deeply rooted in anicent traditions on the island of Sardinia.

Cocoon it in Finland

In The Land of a Thousand Lakes,
where Karelian pasties bake
Suomi winter blows in with bite,
turning the season snowy white.
The sun is there (it does exist),
though in blue north, it's often missed.

On frozen lakes rugged ones search,
fishing to catch grayling and perch.
Others ladle water over stones
to steam saunas that soothe the bones.
They slap birch twigs against their skin—
go to ice holes, and then jump in.

And so the Finns often cocoon
inside their clean and comfy rooms,
watching the reindeer on the run,
while paper yarn balls are handspun.
Midnight sun is gone for a while,
but Lapland's packed with magic guile.

   Some grey moons are made for sleeping.
   Winds are high, the sky is seeping
   darkness through each seam and crack,
   while sunrays melt in to the black.
   Visions of blossoms on the vine
   and milder morns when spring is fine,
   are seen in hues of Northern Lights
   and fires burning on Finnish nights.

Listen in silence to the cold,
see frost flower fields, silver fold.
Now Tulikivi soapstone's lit,
to bathe in warmth and soon forget,
the ever-short December days,
and dream of lilies sweet in May.

Lucky is he, who is to try
in soup, cake, or alongside rye,
the taste of honeyed cloudberries
(found in moss—'yellow raspberries').
So valued is the little fruit,
the laws protect its every root.

And it's true a Finn's spirit sparks,
in evenings slicing through the dark,
when crystal mist along treetops,
glistens softly upon snowdrops.
Midnight sun is gone for a while,
but Lapland's packed with magic guile.

   Some grey moons are made for sleeping.
   Winds are high, the sky is seeping
   darkness through the seams and cracks,
   but life's not dull and never lacks
   winter sports and a starry choir
   where speech is quiet 'round the fire.
   Potato flatbread is buttered right—
   and weather's fine on Finnish nights.

               And so it's been said of Finland,
        'There is no bad weather - only bad clothing.'

Hot Air Balloon

Fuel fills throat
of balloon's envelope.
Propane ignites—flames roar and blast,
propelling it high through sky mass.
Brown wicker basket tilts on past:
    toy-like toothpick telephone poles,
    low-lying-mist, and crops in rows,
    pea-sized oaks, curled shrubs, and shadows.

Champagne sunrise,
strawberry pies,
I float up amidst a cloud plume,
coasting in a hot air balloon
while over California blooms.
    I gingerly lean in to cool air,
    no invasive screens or windows there—
    I am entwined with the atmosphere.

In vague worry,
scoot and flurry
(no parachute, or safety gizmo),
I fear falling to my death below.
I'm a feather in the breadth and flow,
    above dollhouse homes, and dirt roads,
    sage, and musk, and farm trucks with loads,
    a puzzle-scape, and compass combed.

Suspended mid-air —
one more flare
of fire, and I fly without wings —
blending with shades of earthy things,
sailing like a kite on stray string
        away from nectar honey gland,
        or citrus scents through morning bands
        of lemon sun waking dewy land.

Far from tick-tocks
and city blocks,
what would it be to stay aloft
for many days like albatross —
not landing but to glide across
        extensive lengths and to forget
        electricity, chores, walls, debts,
        and anyone I owed regrets?

Ground grows closer
basket falls lower
than big birds circling blue heights
(swift and sound, they flap out of sight).
Drift on down, tail end of billowed flight —
        air escapes when vent releases.
        Descent — bent knees — pilot teases:
        dips, lifts, drops, tips, stops… then eases.

Settle in Cimarron

Suitcase men schemed from the city
with typewriter hands clean and pretty
they threw down seed and drove away
expectin' easy reap on harvest day
while mud-caked farmers tilled the land
there in the flat Oklahoma pan.

Settle in Cimarron a poster said
on land of buffalo grass it read
there's good potential in amber wheat
for men to tend and carry in sheaves
'cause soil's rich, pockets'll be too
here in the south, Great Plains await you.

Grain overgrowth and Depression's pay
merged with dry earth and gusty wind-clay
where thistles raced, tanglin' in wire
and whistles chased a danglin' dirt choir
of gathered and needled tons of sand
in starless noon known as No Man's Land.

Boise City folk would crawl 'long a rope
home to pray, to believe and to hope
repeatin' words while wearin' wet clokes.
'Next year' was the mantra spoken in chokes
'things'll be brighter across this land
and the fields'll flourish as we'd planned.'

And 'ifs' came often amid the absurd
If only was whispered in everyday words:
If only the sky was crystal-clear blue.
If only no breath of any breeze through.
If only the window would lift from pane.
If only cracked ground were pummelled by rain.

The darkest dust storm blotted sun out—
flour-sack faces withstood the drought.
A cursed Black Sunday had thundered through
blackenin' plains and erasin' blue
and lurin' broke souls to hang themselves
when W. P. A. was placed on shelves.

The grey-linens-poor left plains a ghost.
Jalopies drove for California's coast.
'So long...' from the dust bowl the singer sang
'...been good to know yuh' his gui-tar twanged.
And the block headline poster now was gone,
torn, blown away, *Settle in Cimarron*.

A travel back in time
to a life that wasn't mine.
The Dust Bowl
Black Sunday: 14th of April 1935

It's Hot Here in Cancún

Scorching Cancún's a habanero noon
and burns first-skin faces
The sun's wide eyes make lily fair thighs
hide in cabana places
Guitarróns will play near handmade displays
of trinkets and clay pots
Young Latinas braid for few pesos paid
and tame my tangled knots

    I watch vendors walk down
      past tepid baby blue
     Shoulders tan to brown
      here in Quintana Roo

Rust and mustard walls run along the sprawl
of sandy playa shore
Sales-boy near ocean laughs with emotion
at mangoes bought in scores
Men in clipping ease rhythmically prune trees
while distant sails get trimmed
Cloths are reefed or furled in the blithe world
of tempting Caribbean

    I taste lime trickling down
     near sombreros festooned
    Trade winds brush the ground
     of blanca in Cancún

Hand-rolled fat cigars smoked near taco bars
can linger for hours
Sugar-skulls and bread mark *Day of the Dead*
with marigold flowers
Steeped in the heat of marimba beats—
I salt-licked tequila's fire
Folklorico show on edge of the road
sparked my dance desires

        I feel the sun sink down
     when torches light Cancún
          Guava by the pound
     is sold beneath the moon

Sunset appears wiped with Tabasco stripes
above Mariachi sounds
Yucatán birds sing — flapping coloured wings
in palm trees all around
I might come back to Peninsula and jack
and there I'll swim in
bath temps of the sea — a breaststroke's reach
of burly pelicans

      I hear seagulls dip down
    Smell sweet tropical blooms
       It's time I leave now
        Adios dear Cancún

Autumn Train to Wales

Leave from Romsey on a train journey,
a sparrow past vines thick and thorny.
Settled, I revelled in the ride
to Cardiff Central on direct line,
passing a tangle of bramble high
with berries pressed against blue sky.

Through window's view was quietude.
Leaves fell slow in flutters of hues -
scattered patterns ambrosial mellow:
crimson, mango, speckled yellow,
claret, and candy apple bright,
shimmering in September light.

When autumn days had first arrived,
summer's phase took a final stride,
with warm encore and outward bow,
and farmer took to harvest plough.
Rivers flowed in and out of sight,
and slopes of sloes grew plump and ripe.

First I passed tall Salisbury spire,
then Warminster, and country squire,
where scenes seemed like a meadow's parade,
and *Hay Wain* that John Constable made -
(his brushstrokes in wisps of life and wind
painted in warmth around each bend).

Hurrying sights shown fields ablaze,
and green hillocks, and sheep that grazed,
and swells, swallows, and shady spots,
near brickwork, benches, and rooftops,
and creeks for creatures feeling parched,
when the train then called on Dilton Marsh.

I travelled tracks past graveyard homes,
and breadth of unread cracked headstones.
Massive chalk-art *White Horse* appeared,
on Bratton Downs as it has for years,
trimmed in stone on emerald grass:
when Wiltshire was the next I'd passed.

Westbury station had glossed red doors;
platform sign read, *69th Floor.*
I watched a girl kiss a boy goodbye;
a backpacker had his shoe to tie.
I rode up to Bradford-on-Avon,
where people boarded and train was gone.

Delphinium, and drums of hay,
and white linens on clothesline swayed,
and bikers pedalled daisy path,
when engine driver drew up to Bath.
Young and old were coming and going,
ticket holding or suitcase toting.

Ochre sun fell on Temple Meads,
it dappled lanes, and shadowed trees,
streaming 'long Brunel's Great Railway,
though Clifton Bridge was miles away.
Bristol shined as onlookers stood.
Train rolled on to Filton Abbey Wood.

Vegetable allotments, corn-silk threads,
lay in long rows of earthy beds.
At junction, twin-whistle blew its stack,
then switch-diamond on to new track,
to Wales: cross Severn Estuary -
scenes had no need for commentary.

London is a Friend of Mine

Take Bakerloo or Jubilee Line.
Underground, train whistles, and signs.
Show me Dickensian places and times.
London is a good friend of mine.

West End theatre, sip Pimms or wine.
Leicester Square, Soho, pantomime.
Endless choice, flip a coin to decide.
Cross Abbey Road, ride horses in Hyde.

Bethnal Green, a shower of rain.
Oxford Street, Neal's Yard, narrow lanes.
Black round-back taxi pulls over again.
Shakespeare's Globe, Bankside River Thames.

Regent's, Richmond, and Battersea parks.
London Eye, The Pickle, The Shard.
Take chances, draw straws, perhaps choose a card?
Buckingham Palace, changing of guards?

Madame Tussauds, and Sherlock Holmes.
Baker Street, cream tea, English prose.
The Beatles played rooftop on Saville Row.
Wander Kew's botanical show.

Covent Garden, Trafalgar Square.
Tower Bridge, and Notting Hill there.
Quirky Camden has street food to share.
St. Paul's Cathedral, and words of Voltaire.

Bulldog pride, and Churchillian.
The Crown Jewels, Westminster, Big Ben.
Greenwich Meantime has Prime Meridian.
Walk Jack's dark past in the East End.

Make my way to The V&A.
Royal Arts, bronze sculptures, and Tate.
In China Town the pagoda's ornate.
Hear the Proms or watch the Ballet.

Piccadilly or Circle Line?
Underground, tube stations, and chimes.
I've happily wandered many a time.
London remains a good friend of mine.

Trust Alice

Evergreen reaches deep, in the New Forest.

Dormouse sleeps well, while bluebells sing in chorus.

There atop St. Michaels and All Angel's Church,

far up the hill, the steeple soars in Lyndhurst.

Upon unblemished grounds, wild horses roam free,

near Alice Liddell's grave, beneath a tree.

We saw the looking glass (once hung by her bed),

that had sprung White Rabbit stories: 'feed your head'.

Mrs. Hargreaves, 'was displeased', she'd told the world,

'It's a burden to uphold, that little girl'.

Turning on our feet, like Card Soldiers in line,

we marched down the street, at ten minutes to nine.

In the Mad Hatter Tea Room, we ate cream tea

(a small bottle on the table read, 'drink me').

As we sipped our Darjeeling (with milk—a drop),

and indulged in homemade scones (with jam on top),

neither had we seen, smoking Caterpillar tread,

or sighted, white roses that were painted red.

Passing cottages, on a lush English lane,

by vast golden fields, where ripened rapeseed reigns.

Beaulieu River's dogfish do not bark or cry

(but might, if through the prisms of Carroll's eyes).

A sense of that Wonderland truly exists,

in mystical woodlands that can't be dismissed.

There we found trust, at a yesteryear store,

starting with notes, on Farm Shop's splintered door:

'Sorry! We're closed for business every Sunday.'

'Return! We're open Monday through Saturday.'

Outside that shut shop, fresh eggs were in a tub

(and across the road, was The Leaky Taps pub).

Beside grey cartons, was a cash box on twine,

non-tethered, unlocked, with a handwritten sign:

'Please put pound and pence in—£1.60 for six'

(I dropped my coins and then chose a varied-mix).

Ah yes! The honour system, faith, and mercy!

If only the whole world, was that trustworthy!

Freight Trains in Idaho

T-t-twang it does go an' d-dang if he ever knowed
                    why passenger trains run sssmooth,
a-movin' like a greased groove
                    and freight trains r-r-rumble
and sho 'nuff narr'ly tumble
                    off Idaho rail tracks
where field taters're tossed 'ta sacks
                    that are rough bags of burlap
used fo' summer games p'haps
                    at lake picnics by the mission
where he be fish-fishin'
                    o' lay on street corner bends
fo' po' boys ta sit on them
                    an' one-two-three pitch pennies
an' scratch out tunes a-many.

-ch-choo-ch-ch-choo-ch-ch-choo-ch-ch-choo-ch-ch-choo-ch-ch-choo-

Yeah, b-boing-boing rubber bands
                    an' b-bang-bang top o' cans
an' maybe go a-slip-slappin'
                    an' do some toe-tappin'
in shoes which got no laces,
                    but do fine in all places
like where barefoot Billy Karp
                    goes s-solo on mouth-harp
an' big black Buster Chevy
                    he done always thump heavy
s-s-scrunchin' his face
                    on his grandpa's b-boomin' bass
while skinny E. Sam McGrune
                    can slam-bam out a tune
an' his bird arms go flappin'
                    when those cool pipes a-happen.

-ch-ch-choo-ch-ch-choo-ch-ch-choo-ch-ch-choo-ch-ch-choo-ch-ch-choo-

Train whistles b-blowin'
                'cross Indian corn a-growin'
they's dawn crackin' noisy
                h-howlin' outta Boise
an' ol' Skip Cal Leevy
                in his dog dirty dungarees
loves h-hoppin' a freight ride,
                dern takin' it in s-stride
findin' fleein' excitin'
                when hot damn it's invitin'
yeah them box cars they's rusty
                p-pushin' 'long the dusty
sidewindin' egg bakin'
                B & O freedom takin' line
passin' junkyards an' barbed wire
                an' factories with smoke fire.

-ch-choo-ch-ch-choo-ch-ch-choo-ch-ch-choo-ch-ch-choo-ch-ch-choo-

Skip Cal spits and he don't gripe,
                lax with grimy drifter types
smokin' cigs an' eatin' beans,
                next to men in oily jeans
when I-dee-ho crop so cream,
                paves way in a young boy's dream
chasin' freights that r-rumble,
                an' sho 'nuff narr'ly tumble.
Diesel smell done chokes a horse;
                Skip he aint got no remorse
carvin' words with pocket knife,
                'long side cars when day is bright.
Damn he oughtta be in school,
                but Skip lives by Skip's own rules.

-ch-ch-choo-ch-ch-choo-ch-ch-choo-ch-ch-choo-ch-ch-choo-ch-ch choo-

Ye'sir,
      whistles an' chug-a-chug steam…
              it's all jus' a young boy's dream.
              It's all jus' a young boy's dream.

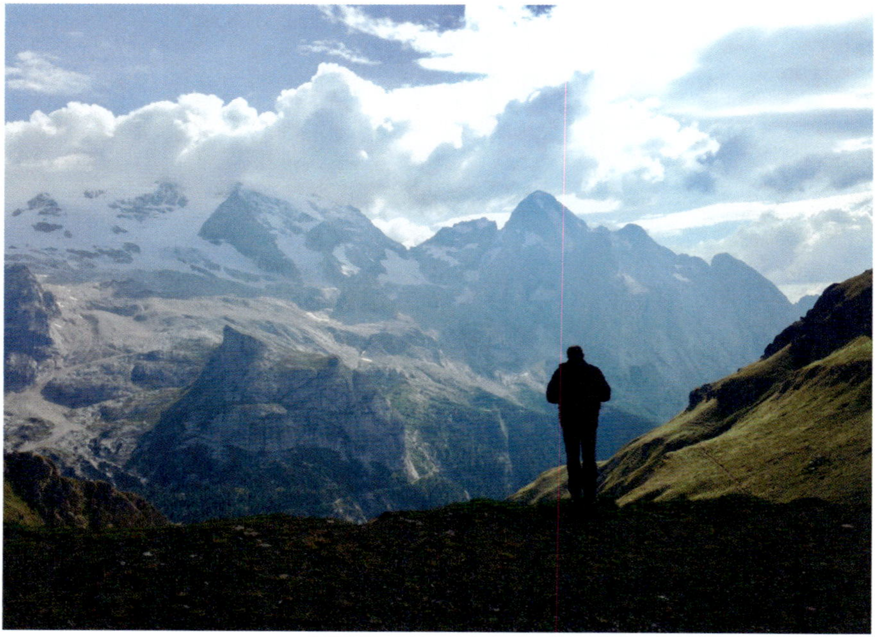

Hold Tight Dolomites (for Northern Italy)

Hold tight Dolomites.
I'll cleave, disinclined to leave
your Alps, lakes and trees,

your far starlit peaks
shading wolds and gold broomrape,
on bold massif-scape,

where boats row slowly
on mirrored flows reflecting
mist evanescence,

and black grouse and owls
prowl near mountains that don't move...
but hard rocks can bruise,

due to observing
changes and unnerving sights.
Hold tight Dolomites.

Schloss Neuschwanstein 'New Swan-on-the-rock Castle' is legendary. It's an architectural wonder, often regarded as the world's most magnificent castle—a jewel in Bavaria's crown.

Neuschwanstein in the Clouds

We'd left Baden-Baden and our days in the Black Forest—
how morish - eating fresh doughy pretzels along the ride.
Romantic Road drive - etched golden rays through
        a breadth of pale.

It was floating ethereally on white-feathered brows -
in clouds - the sunbeams spotlighted the castle in the air.
A sky's prayer - Schloss Neuschwanstein rose
        like a fairytale.

It's a storybook-scape from the Alps to the Danube plain -
like rolling skeins - knitter's greens in verdant pastures rich.
The footbridge bewitched - over Pöllat Gorge and
        the broadness.

Below sky's blue dome stood Bavaria's theatrical -
the castle - inspired by notes of Wagner's music.
'Shy Ludwig' lavished and embellished
        in utter excess.

Present day fades away where the lederhosen still sells -
and cowbells - simple things that faintly ring will mesmerize
Aggrandize - it's fair, when every aspect
        seeks attention.

There are times when one feels so small in a prodigious place
- the sheer space - of that castle, that land, the mountains, and
lakes, makes me retake - breathless dream spells,
        merely at its mention.

Luray Caverns, Virginia, USA

Hushpuppies and Grits

'Yes Ma'am', said a man in the cabin, 'we've plenty'.
I then emptied out a pocketful of pennies.
At a barstool I sat eating hushpuppies and grits.
I squeezed a plastic bear, and its ranger hat dripped
sourwood honey onto crisp morning toast.

In the Blue Ridge Mountains along Skyline Drive's bow
American Dogwood—Cornus Florida grows.
Up in the Smokies 'cross the Appalachian Trail
I watched as Audubon's exotic birds set sail:
the barn swallow, the thrasher, the common starling.

Soft static filled the radio while music played
a down-home bluegrass gospel called 'I'll Fly Away',
when a gold Kentucky warbler rested her wings
on a sugar maple glistening in misty morning's
sunbeams on wild dewberries near a white-tailed fawn.

Shenandoah burst in vibrant foliage of flames
near celestial river and speckled country lanes,
and Luray Caverns blasted songs on stalacpipe
in hidden caves of stalactites and stalagmites,
where I finished a bag of crispy hushpuppies.

Where Golden Fields Rush Kansas

*Sweepin' plains of Kansas, beneath stars,
beneath patriotic stripes too.
Ancestral farm lies on amber fields of grain.
Peace an' joy—Granny Smith apple pies,
coolin' on opened-shutter chipped sill
beside pantry lined with State Fair jams:
first prize ribbons hang 'cross berry labels.*

*Mighty oaks with a kinship I've known
through childhood days into seasoned years
held tire swings when troubles were none
where accordion shaped lights were strung
swayin' multi-coloured party bright
shadin' supper tables, skimmin' roofs
durin' grace's folded hands, heads bowed.*

*Oh the Red Flyer wagons we pulled
kickin' dust onto Ma's laundry line.
Cottons scrubbed, I was soap-cake clumsy.
Skinny arms, tight braids, knobby knees,
never mind the gap-toothed crooked smile
or the fact that I couldn't hold a tune.
Beauty queen, never be, though blessed indeed.*

*I've relished watermelon picnics
in ruffled ginghams an' straw hats,
summer eve's barn dances an' fiddle fests,
twilight fireflies tremblin' under glass-
pickle jar lanterns for hide an' seek,
an' pre-teen kisses upon flushed cheeks.
Moon's pearly shine lit my freckled face.*

*The white daisy wedding was to come,
my hair flowin' long, loose, angelic blonde.
Soon barefoot with babes: one, two, three,
but the fourth one born, oh heat brought forth
violent fever that made me dig her grave.
Mother Mary gave strength for a fifth child—
he'd hardly a reason to cough or sneeze.*

*Twister stripped land in '57—
it took my tractor borne husband then.
I cursed the clouds once, so unlike me.
Lean years were met with oatmeal stretched.
Scrambled egg dishes we'd thank the Lord
for three small hens who'd escaped the winds
an' for roosters crowin' each sunrise.*

*Beatin' rag rugs in clove autumntide
my sunken grey eyes held back the pain
of arthritic hands, dry an' pin-pricked.
Needlepoint pillows, homemade trinkets
earned dollars and pennies, by an' by.
Blinked my eyes—four children grown an' gone.
I wear lacy sunflower print aprons.*

*Absent whispers—it's too lonesome now—
a full house mingles at Christmastime only.
My brood's got me packin' for Hawaii,
near sand, an' a rattan bed an' fan.
Waves an' seashells I'm aimin' to see.
Maybe I'll be bakin' with pineapple.
Clear thinkin'—mine aint so straight no more.*

*I'd wished for plum hardy ones to tend
Great Grandfather's overlooked wheat fields.
Christian I am—Almighty I trust—
He has His plan set out for me.
On my porch, without complaints, I'll rock,
soaked in a century of memories,
despisin' nothin'... but the For Sale sign.*

Open Market in Winchester

Here in the land of Jane Austen
nettle's sting me on the landing,
(Mizmaze, on St. Catherine's Hill),
where St. Swithun was once standing.

Homemade jam and fat piggy ham-
I choose scones, fatty cream, and fruit,
and spill 'long Winch's cobbled paths,
pass kettle sign, and Cobbler's boot.

Cherries-red and blueberries-blue —
vendors sell from berry barrows,
while buskers sing-song for spare pence,
and Cathedral boys sing like sparrows.

Alfred the Great statue stands guard
by the bus-stand and the Guildhall.
Debtors' old prison: Westgate Arch,
is the gateway to The Great Hall.

Mill wheel rolls on teal Itchen River.
Men fish for teal on Meadow's stream.
I pass Wolvsey Castle ruins,
to pass time with my scone and cream.

Milky tea of loose Earl Grey leaves,
at Market beneath a milk sky.
Time for home, though my brolley broke.
British weather's broken (I sigh).

Bruges, Belgium

Crow-stepped gables, Baroque art, and gothic hall,
I drifted past pert tulips, and poppies small,
down Goudenhand canal in an open boat,
where a blonde dog in an upper window sprawled.

After eating a waffle with strawberries,
I'd climbed eighty-two metres up the Belfry,
under broken skies over Grote Markt crowd,
when forty-seven bells rang in a tarry.

Flanders sunshine can quickly turn to raining,
then swiftly switch back with the clouds all fading,
so I ducked through a door at Groeningemuseum,
for Hieronymus Bosch, and van Eyck paintings.

I tasted Belgian chocolates—hand-dipped couverture,
I passed wood houses, leaded windows, and mortar,
in cake-icing-polychrome old town Bruges — then,
humpback bridges called me back to the water.

Modern Times in Ancient Egypt

Phantom Pharaohs seemingly outlast hot desert sands so freely
turning and sun-burning me.
Skies stretch wide with no divide between the bands of arid land
reminding me how small I am.

Idolized Great Sphinx of Giza sits faithfully for timeless days
revered as god of harvest's fate.
Colossal lion-man of stone with broken nose
keeps shepherd's watch
on Plateau's sweep of grand mirage.

Tassels waft breezily upon my one-hump dromedary
rising tall on knobby-knees.
Hint of myrrh tops dorsal fur on ride to pyramids so high
they pierce the empyrean skies.

    Arabesque dress. Linens long.
    Oh all the countless hues of prisms beyond the blues.
    How many colours has the world?
    How many colours has the world?

Daily chants sound out on amps when busy roads of Cairo flow
while constant noise of car horns blow.
Saqqara bound for Funerary Grounds where green does not exist
amidst the hushed necropolis.

Mystic powers of lotus flowers sail along the Nile and veer
into the Dead Sea atmosphere.
Citadel reflects its gilt on to a hill of jasmine blossoms
that loom like jewels of Tutankhamen.

There's aromatic syriac, hand-sewn leather ottomans,
and cotton, and kyphi incense.
Mosaic lamps follow faces tracing light on hieroglyphs
and brass spittoons and Eye of Horus.

Peddling in tangled traffic young men balance trays of tea
and pour for morning drivers' needs.
Beauty contrasts dire things like poverty in empty eyes
infesting tears with droves of flies.

    Arabesque dress. Linens long.
    I can't ignore the hues—all the emotional blues.
    How many colours has the world?
    How many colours has the world?

Sequoiadendron Giganteum

If I had my own way — (Sequoias in a hideaway)
I would meditate on cool moss once a day,
imagining stories trees have overheard and viewed,
within thousands of years that carried on through.
I'd give praise to that Northern California Park—
while pressing my hands along rough knotted bark,
and I'd be grateful for breath-giving trees there,
by smothering my senses in that redwood air.

If I'd my own way I'd listen to the General Sherman tree —
perhaps earth's largest redwood might tell me:
'**Awl leafed branches aren't strung with lights or swings,
but our energy gives life to all living things**'.
At the Gem of the Sierras (called **Crescent Meadow**)—
I'd fall on my knees and whisper to trees I don't know,
'**Why were you once cut to matchsticks and posts?!
Why had greedy people felled Giants, down to ghosts?**'

If my way was possible, forever redwoods would stay,
and I'd hope for humans to thank John Muir and say,
'**We respect you. The planet is in need of those
who'll follow in protecting wilderness abodes**'.
It's captivating that all trees can translate
(to a degree) knowledge of the forest and its fate.
Learning from nature's ways of comprehension,
should be reason enough for mankind's attention.

Venice Simplon-Orient-Express

Venice, Italy: In the piazza Vivaldi's music played. Days were on the lace-making island of Burano, the glass-making island of Murano, the cemetery island of San Michele, running high up San Marco's campanile, drinking strong espresso by the Grand Canal, and watching as the gilded sun slipped down. Drifting in a gondola past Rialto Bridge...we then walked tirelessly through countless passages.

Santa Lucia station: On the platform for the outbound. An old-fashioned band of uniformed men blew tones—blasting away on cornets, trumpets, and trombones. The crew greeted us beside the train's gold-trimmed blue, they looked smart and sharp, pouring Prosecco into flutes. White-gloved porters stepped us back to the golden age: to glamour, luxury, and corridors of parquet. Authentic 1920s style was there to impress. Oh that wondrous Venice Simplon-Orient-Express!

Twin berth: Rupert was our steward, and eased open the door. There were banquette sofas, bone china, and art deco fans. And robes, velvet slippers, and a water flask to hand. Near to a bright and blossoming yellow bouquet, a grandfatherly washbasin was neatly tucked away. Suitcases were placed in an antique luggage rack; next to oak panelling, we both settled back.

(continued)

Venice Simplon-Orient-Express

Peace: Curled up near windows, we watched a series of tall grasses. Alps were collared in May snow, with blanketed white patches. Scenes changed frequently from Dolomites, to flocks of sheep, past Verona, past cottages, past firs on open green. Passing through Innsbruck, we snacked on a bonne bouche treat: muffins, biscuits, and an assortment of teas. The train, through winding turns, somehow seemed to narrate. With rocking chair wisdom, it did its best to translate.

Mingle: While reading Christie's *Murder*, enchanted views came—like an artist's fine paintings shifting in a frame. Tipping and leaning as we strolled through every car, we heard cakewalks and rags at the piano bar. All around us was opaque glass and art nouveau. La Monde news rested on tables basked in pink glow. The modern and digital, were left behind—porters used pocket-watches to check on the time. Each steward was soft spoken; each one was well versed. They stepped aside, let us by, nicely unrehearsed. Carriages had carried dignitaries, statesmen, and royalty: Queen Elizabeth, Winston Churchill, and Jackie Kennedy.

Dinner: Dressing was a balancing bit of ballet: first position, fifth position, demi-plié. There was bumping and laughter and a time to learn, when holding ourselves up through many twists and turns. We dined in Étoile du Nord car with stunning marquetry, and echoes of alpine edelweiss, fresh and ivory. Some dined in L'Oriental car that shined in black lacquer. Others dined near Lalique friezes in the Côte d'Azur. Yes the cuisine was exquisite and Michelin star, but scenery took first prize, undoubtedly, by far. We had private sights of gentle, breezy, and tame—most which goes unseen by automobile or plane. In precarious moments, the train scraped the edge. It managed to stay upright when riding the ledge. It snaked through chasms, and the tight and narrow—past ravines, past chalets, past steeples, and yarrow. When sun set on Lake Geneva, the passengers gushed. It glistened with radiance of sparkling diamond dust.

Sleep: There was a velvety ladder, and taffeta shades, and the foldaway beds with damask sheets were made. The rumble was a lullaby rocking steadily. Along the rails, beneath the floor, wheels churned endlessly. And when off in slumber of faraway stories, I heard the train whispering of timeless glories. In the wee small hours when spring's rainfall tapped—those seventeen carriages stopped still on a track.

Morning rise: Breakfast arrived. Buttery sun streamed softly through the corridor, and played upon the gloss of polished wooden floors. There came a whistlestop, for wine and Paris break—then back to the dining car—lunch and berry cake.

Finale: A coach through the Eurotunnel, and back to Britain—to ride on a sister-train—the British Pullman. In big overstuffed chairs we had scones and champagne. We ate finger sandwiches, and pushed home again. I longed to remember all of the smooth details—never to forget the train, the views, and the rails. I read somewhere, about the finest train on earth -
I agree to the letter: *Venice Simplon-Orient-Express—
the train against which all trains are measured.*

The Simplon—the world's second longest rail tunnel (Switzerland-Italy).

Train Travel

I've covertly **taken looks**
I've *sometimes* **stealthily stared**
I've slyly **peered over books**
I've occasionally **glared**
At the **passengers I've seen**
For whom I'd **invented names**
Imagining **varied dreams**
Of strangers **in carriage frames**
Spied on in *smeared* **reflections**
And dated seats **in tired rows**
Blind to my brief **inspections**
Of faces **in train windows**

Down the Mighty Mississippi (for Samuel Clemens)

Chance on the ghost of Samuel, down by muddy river,
shinin' up a gold timepiece, his pockets full of silver.
He's in shade sippin' lemonade, wearin' a cotton suit,
coolin' his head 'long Delta bed, scuffin' his leather boot
on swamp rocks 'longside jawharps, his words write out like hymns
'bout Old Man (that river grand), and a character named Jim.

Paddlewheel goes off the reel, rollin' in incessant flow
like whiskey, rye, southern sighs, and when calliope blows
for Choctaw and Chickasaw tribes of the Mississippi
where Huck Finn jumped a raft and then, hollered somethin' lippy.

Sam was a steamboat pilot and his spirit lurks there still,
from Northern Minnesota to where Louisiana spills
into the Gulf of Mexico and deep Pacific Sea,
where witty Clem clam-baked plans 'bout a houseboy runnin' free.
In the Sound the ripple's calm, at two fathoms safe -'mark twain'.
Because of love of river's worth, he fondly penned that name.

Hear banjoes playin' low, and go ride the Mississippi,
smack between the east and west in the land of liberty.
Try fried tomatoes, Cajun slaw, spiced chitlins, ribs and beans,
peppered crab legs, oyster sauce, and most surely collard greens.
Forget your swags, and wave your flag, the one that Betsy sewed,
and get a fill in Hannibal of Clemens' boyhood home.

Perhaps just once, for love of Twain, sail the Mighty if you can,
past buttonbush, and bulrush hills, awed by the expanse.
Yes maybe once, for dear ol' Mark, ride the river if you can,
past magnolia and mayhaw, awed by the expanse.

For Miss Honduras

In Honduras there are plantains and bananas strung,
and passion fruit in heaps upon tin barrows,
on every corner where the traffic's slow,
        and the mangoes sell—very well.

On the shores the little girls are selling beaded bands—
I gladly pay a fee for two or three,
while the vendors squat on sandy feet,
        in the winter sun—'til their day is done.

At Half Moon Bay I met a shopkeeper with dusty shelves,
wearing shirt and shorts in need of a good clean.
He watched tourists haggle with their green,
        over things for sale—like plastic pails.

Beyond white beaches, and Rain of Fish phenomenon,
past the orchids, in the jungle is a man—
he's on a hammock near a grand toucan,
        and I had to stare—at the keel-billed there.

See the divers in the Maya blue Caribbean
and the shopkeeper eat his cheese and beans
when the sun turns into tangerine,
        spider monkey sits—with me a bit.

The little girls are dressed alike and they wave goodbye,
off to school beginning well into the day.
They take their brother's hands and race away,
        as I stop a while—to give a smile.

        Roatan—I will long—remember you.
        High—I zip-lined through your skies of blue
        (the ones Miss Honduras knew).

Women dance the punta barefoot as maracas shake,
while the men are beating congas rhythmically,
then scuba boat returns from Barrier Reef,
        but small joys aside—there are hidden cries.

There is evil lurking and it goes without resolve,
like with the criminals who slayed Maria Josè.
Miss Honduras was blown away,
        and her sister too—this is nothing new.

Only three percent of cases come to closure there.
In just one year: five-hundred thirty-one
women dead and gone, but what's been done?
        Police turn away—happens every day.

By the aqua seas it seems there's peace in everyone,
but in truth—seven hundred souls unclaimed.
Secrets, lies, and not a one is blamed
        for the bloody knives—or loss of lives.

Crime is rampant, yet the people live in fear of God,
and for simple things like fishing Yojoa Lake,
or sitting on their porch with yucca cake.
        And Christians sing—love is everything.

        Roatan—I will long—remember you.
        High—I zip-lined through your skies of blue
        (the ones Miss Honduras knew).

Pretty girls, beauty queens, were disappearing. Honduras has sharply contrasting sides: one is the lush green jungle, balmy weather, families living simple lives set against a clear turquoise ocean; the other is (at the time of writing this book) it's one of the leading places in the world, for homicide.

The art
     is all around you

Chantilly, France

Le Château de Chantilly
is snowy-white and story-like
and ever-tempting as gateau.
Medieval castle—fortress home,
steel-grey dormers and ashen domes,
with silver swans swimming the moat.

Tall lime trees bend in canopy
like a veil over love's shy bride
they whisper, rustle and echo,
trill and tremolo low in winds,
singing in strings of violins
softly played by Cupid's arrow.

Sweet Chantilly cream, and fine
delicate threads of blonde noire,
and differing timeless treasures:
Ingres, and Delacroix,
and a rose garden and boudoir,
and whispers of freed downy feathers.

On paths leading up to seven towers
nearly ruined and then restored,
waterfalls spill on fairy lawns
by woods of aristocracy
near horses in Grande Ecuries
beside eighteenth century ponds.

Kayaking in Nova Scotia

I dreamt of honeycomb and simple things

(momentarily wrapped in a daydream),

when the Atlantic's cold ocean woke me,

while up in Nova Scotia kayaking.

Pointed boats in electric colours met

at shoreline: lime green, yellow, sapphire blue.

The glass paddles circled, slapped, and splashed through

icy sea, white caps, calm coves, and inlet.

Eagles and osprey flew Halifax sky

over rocky ledges and fishing shacks—

they flapped above trusty cockpit kayaks

alongside random chatters from magpie.

My rhythmic pace tapped in sync with the sea—

where earth, faint eddies, and lapping waves blend

with intrinsic voices I heard, and then

was land bound for warm hodge podge, and tea.

Haiku for Holland

Windmill sails churn blue

Windlust pivot, so must I

In wind, tulips bend

Wander On

He's somewhere (what does he know),
he wanders pillar to post
sand inside his shoes and only pennies for some toast.
He roams—
one day hauling grapes, or pulling tape,
or maybe stacking up a host
of expensive things he doesn't care to own.

He's picking blackberries or pacing concrete aisles
stealing ferry rides to places he'll see within his trials.
He'll go far—
sail away, he'll build a gate, and keep a smile for a while
he's rootless yet he's tangled like a vine.

>All of the world
>the world out there has such despair
>but he will find his peace
>and his piece of life is waiting just for him.

He speaks fast like wind within his gift of gab wide grin—
he's shifting moving slowly never finding his own win.
He's alone—
a passenger in homes and cars of those who pay him thin
with rides or meals or boozy offerings.

His sleeves are rolled while washing bowls
in Joe's Café Sweet
he says, 'Place to place, I earn stays and a little bit to eat'.
He's in need—
of something more than eyes can see
more than a gash could ever bleed,
ah he—he pretends to be content.

    All of the world
    the world out there hasn't time to spare
    yet he will find his peace
    and his piece of life is waiting just for him.

He is where high tide comes in and fishermen lay bounds
of seafood stuff to be cut up,
or thrown against the ground.
He's tired—
as he mops fish blood and trudges scruffy boots
where he is found
he's off again and searching for the sun.

He muscles mounds of dirt and shovels gravel
'long the streets
tipping newsboy cap at strangers he consequently meets.
His weary soul—
unravelling and babbling 'bout sores upon his feet
when he gains her heart it's something to believe.

    All of the world
    the world out there has love to share
    and he has found his peace
    and his piece of life was waiting just for him.

Peace in life was waiting just for him.

Acknowledgements -

Frank Lloyd Wright - 1867-1959

Kahlil Gibran -1883-1931

I Wandered Lonely as a Cloud - by William Wordsworth - first published 1807

'*Chattanooga Choo-Choo*'- 1941- written and composed by Mack Gordon/Harry Warren

'*So Long, It's Been Good to Know Yuh*' - released 1935 - written by Woodie Guthrie

The Hay Wain - by John Constable - 1921

Alice Pleasance Liddell Hargreaves - 1852-1934
Alice's Adventures in Wonderland - 1865- by Lewis Carroll

Richard Wagner - 1813-1833

The Adventures of Tom Sawyer - 1884
by Samuel Clemens, a.k.a., Mark Twain

United Nations Office on Drugs and Crime 2018-
Honduras: highest homicide rates of all countries of the world

George Bernard Shaw -1856-1950

Thank-you:
To my beloved husband, Mark, for a lifetime of standing beside me; to my precious children, Kanan, Bo, and Dusty, for encouraging and supporting me along the way; to my wonderful parents Neil and Evelyn, for inspiring travel at an early age; to The Beatles, for helping shape my life and for being part of my identity; and for my dearest friends that I feel lucky to have found in this wide world.